Super Science Experiments

MURIEL MANDELL

Illustrated by Dave Garbot

STERLING

New York / London
www.sterlingpublishing.com/kids

No-Sweat Science is a trademark of Sterling Publishing Co., Inc.

STERLING and the distinctive Sterling logo are registered trademarks of Sterling Publishing Co., Inc.

Library of Congress Cataloging-in-Publication Data Available

10   9   8

Published by Sterling Publishing Co., Inc.
387 Park Avenue South, New York, NY 10016
© 2005 by Sterling Publishing Co., Inc.
Previously published as *Simple Science Experiments with Everyday Materials*, © 1989 by Muriel Mandell
Distributed in Canada by Sterling Publishing
c/o Canadian Manda Group, 165 Dufferin Street
Toronto, Ontario, Canada M6K 3H6
Distributed in the United Kingdom by GMC Distribution Services
Castle Place, 166 High Street, Lewes, East Sussex, England BN7 1XU
Distributed in Australia by Capricorn Link (Australia) Pty. Ltd.
P.O. Box 704, Windsor, NSW 2756, Australia

Sterling ISBN-13: 978-1-4027-2149-6
         ISBN-10: 1-4027-2149-8

For information about custom editions, special sales, premium and corporate purchases, please contact Sterling Special Sales Department at 800-805-5489 or specialsales@sterlingpub.com.

For Horace and Mark and Jonathan,
who have continued to be collaborators.

CONTENTS

BEFORE YOU BEGIN

Ordinary materials can be used in extraordinary ways. And that's exactly what you do in the experiments in this book—you taste electricity with a lemon, make a water trombone with a straw, use a spot of butter to tell which lightbulb is brighter, and more and more.

We chose these experiments because they are fun and easy to do and because they explain interesting scientific principles. They get you thinking about science in a different way. They also *work*—we were amazed at how many experiments in science books *don't.* They're safe, too. You won't be dealing with dangerous materials or need to use an open flame or house current. A few of them call for a stove, and those are labeled *HOT!* You can see them at a glance and get help, if that's the rule at your house.

It's a good idea to set aside a special corner or shelf for the odds and ends you'll be using. A shoebox makes a good storage bin. You might want to keep a notebook to jot down what you do and what happens.

Don't be discouraged if an experiment doesn't seem to work. Read over the instructions and try it again. You'll probably spot the problem right away. Often you learn more from "failing" than you do when everything goes right.

The simpler experiments are at the beginning of each chapter, but you can start anywhere without reading what comes before.

Have fun—and amaze your friends—with these ordinary things that aren't so ordinary!

CLUTCHING AT STRAWS

An ordinary drinking straw can become an atomizer, a medicine dropper, an oboe or trombone, a scale—and more!

ABOUT STRAWS

What is a straw? The dictionary defines it as a stalk or stem of dried, threshed grain, such as wheat, rye, oats, or barley. The first drinking straws were cut from stalks of grain. That's how they got their name.

The first paper straw was patented in 1888 by Marvin Chester Stone of Washington, D.C. It was rolled by hand from manila paper and coated with paraffin.

Drinking straws were handmade until 1905, when Stone's company invented the first successful straw-making machine.

Now drinking straws are made of paper or plastic and sometimes glass.

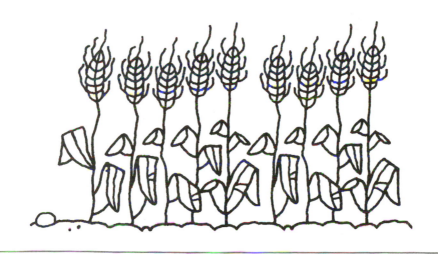

How Does a Straw Work?

Do you think you use a straw to pull liquid up into your mouth? Not so!

You need:

a drinking straw
a glass of water
a jar (or empty glass)

WHAT TO DO:

Put the straw into the glass of water. Hold your finger over the top of the straw and take the straw out of the liquid. Place the straw over the jar. Then remove your finger from the top of the straw.

WHAT HAPPENS:

While your finger covers the top of the straw, the liquid remains in the straw. When you remove your finger, the water flows out.

WHY:

Your finger on top of the straw lessens the pressure of the air from above the straw. The greater pressure of air under the straw holds the liquid inside it.

When you suck through a straw, you are not actually pulling the liquid up. What you are really doing is removing some of the air inside the straw. This makes the pressure inside the straw lower than the pressure outside. The greater pressure of the outside air then pushes the liquid in the glass up through the straw and into your mouth.

A pipette, a tube scientists use to measure and transfer a liquid from one container to another, works the same way.

Making a Paper Straw

Cut out a strip of paper 2 inches by 10 inches (5 cm x 25 cm). Holding the paper at one corner, start rolling it diagonally in a narrow cylinder shape until it is all rolled up. Then fasten the sides with tape.

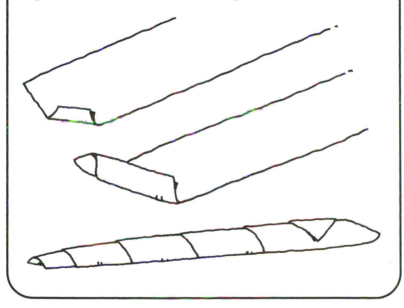

Straw Atomizer

This is the way window-cleaning sprays and perfume atomizers work.

You need:
a straw
a glass of water
scissors

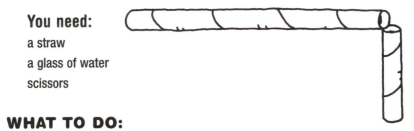

WHAT TO DO:

About one-third of the distance from one end of the straw, cut a horizontal slit. Bend the straw at the slit and slip the short section into a glass of water, keeping the slit about $1/4$ inch (6 mm) above the surface of the water.

Blow hard through the long section of the straw.

WHAT HAPPENS:

Water enters the straw from the glass and comes out through the slit as a spray.

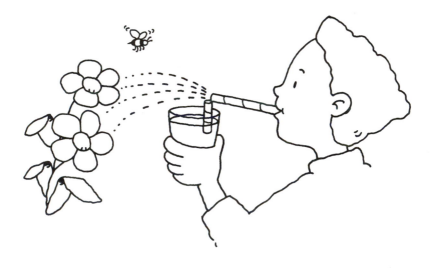

WHY:

As you blow through the long section of the straw, a stream of air flows over the top of the short section, reducing the pressure at that point. As normal pressure underneath forces water up into the straw, the moving air blows it off in drops. In atomizers and spray cans, you use a pump to blow in air.

Making a Medicine Dropper

You can make a regular drinking straw into a medicine dropper. Put a straw into a glass of liquid. Hold it in the straw by covering the top of the straw with your finger. Then bend your finger slightly and raise and lower your fingertip so that the liquid flows out one drop at a time. Experiment with the straw until you get the knack of it. It's easy to do.

Straw Oboe

You can make music with a straw. The first wind instruments were probably hollow reeds picked and played by shepherds in the field.

You need:
a straw
scissors

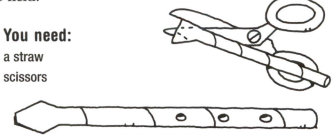

WHAT TO DO:

Pinch flat ½ to ¾ inch (12–19 mm) of a straw at one end. Cut off little triangles from the corners to form reeds. Put the straw far enough into your mouth so that your lips don't touch the corners. Don't pucker your lips, but blow hard. Cut three small slits along the length of the straw an inch or so apart. Separate the slits so that they form small round holes. Cover one of them and blow. Then cover two, then three, blowing each time.

WHAT HAPPENS:

Each time you blow, you hear a different sound. You can play simple tunes by covering and uncovering the holes.

WHY:

As in a real oboe, the two wedges—called reeds—opening and closing at high speed first allow air to flow into the straw and then stop the flow. Vibrating air crates the sound. As you cover and uncover the holes, you regulate the length of the air column, and that determines the pitch. The shorter the air column, the faster it vibrates and the higher the note.

Make a Water Trombone

With a soda bottle, some water, and a straw, you can make a slide trombone.

You need:

a straw
water
a soda bottle

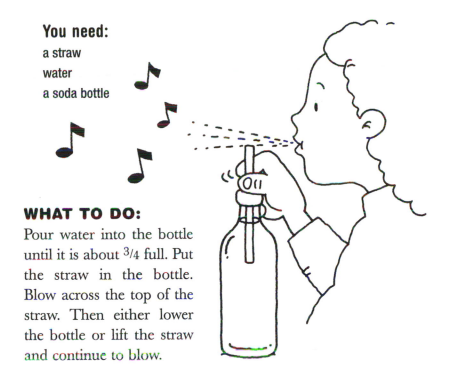

WHAT TO DO:

Pour water into the bottle until it is about 3/4 full. Put the straw in the bottle. Blow across the top of the straw. Then either lower the bottle or lift the straw and continue to blow.

WHAT HAPPENS:

As you lower the bottle, the sound gets lower in pitch.

WHY:

You are lengthening the column of air in the straw. This is how a slide trombone works.

Bend a Straw Without Touching It

You can "bend" a straw without touching it!

You need:
a straw
a glass or jar of water

WHAT TO DO:
Place the straw in a glass half-filled with water. Look at it from the top, bottom, and sides.

WHAT HAPPENS:
When you look at the straw from the side of the glass, it appears to be bent or broken at the point where it enters the water.

WHY:
We see an object because rays of light come to our eyes from it. Light rays travel more slowly through glass and water than through air. Therefore, light from the part of the straw in the water reaches our eyes later than the part that is above the water, and the straw appears bent.

Spear a Potato

Would you think an ordinary drinking straw could pierce a potato without destroying itself?

You need:

a raw baking potato
several paper straws

WHAT TO DO:

If the potato is old, soak it in water for a half hour or so before trying this experiment. Then, with one fast, strong push, thrust the straw straight down into the potato.

WHAT HAPPENS:

The straw pierces the potato without buckling or bending.

WHY:

Inertia is the tendency of objects to continue whatever they are doing. An object at rest (the potato) tends to remain at rest while an object that is moving (the straw) tends to keep moving in the same direction.

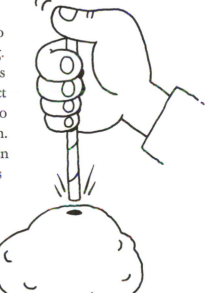

Straws from the field have been driven into—and through—planks of wooden barns and houses when propelled by tornado-force winds.

Straw Wheels

Do wheels make work easier? See for yourself.

You need:
2 to 4 straws

a book

WHAT TO DO:
Place a book on the table and try to push it. Then place the straws on the table and put the book on top of the straws. Push the book.

WHAT HAPPENS:
Without the straws, you need to push hard to move the book. With the straws, the book moves more easily.

WHY:
When one item rubs against another, it resists moving because both surfaces are not completely smooth. The bumps of one surface (the book) catch against the bumps in the other (the table). The amount of this resistance, known as friction, depends on the kinds of surfaces and the forces pressing them together. The rougher the surfaces, the greater the friction. Rolling results in less friction than sliding.

Straw Balance Scale

This balance can actually be a real scale. All you have to do is to calibrate it—figure out what its movements mean by checking out items whose weight you already know.

You need:

a straw

a small paper cup or
  deep, narrow cardboard box

scissors

a pencil or pen

a pencil eraser cap
  or lump of clay

a large needle

an index card

a large spool of thread

WHAT TO DO:

Make two oblong notches on opposite sides of the paper cup, or cut down parts of two ends of the cardboard box. (See A.)

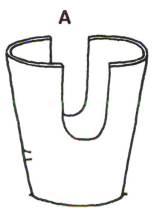

A

Cut away part of one end of a straw to form a little scoop. (See B.) Fit the eraser cap on the other end of the straw. Pad it with a little paper if it is too large. (See C.)

Push the needle through one side of the cup, then through the marked spot of the straw, then through the other end of the cup. Pull out the eraser head a little so that the straw slants slightly upward. (See D on page 20.)

B

C

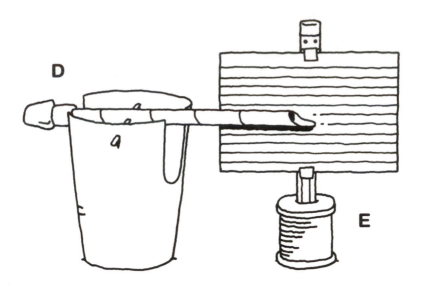

Tape the index card or a strip of cardboard to a pencil or pen and stand it in the spool. Place the spool so that the straw's scoop falls across the index card. (See E.)

Your scale is finished! Try it out by placing a few grains of sugar in the scoop, or by hanging a paper clip from it.

WHAT HAPPENS:

The straw moves down.

WHY:

Your scale is a lever. It acts like a seesaw. The place at which the level rests (the needle) is called the fulcrum. When the straw lies flat, the distance and the weight on one side of the needle balance out the distance and the weight on the other side. As you add weight, you change the relationship between the two sides of the needle.

Finding the Center of Gravity

Figure out the point at which the straw balances. Do this by hanging the straw on the spine of a book or on the edge of an upright metal ruler. Move the straw about until it doesn't fall off. It will probably be fairly close to the eraser. Mark that point of balance with a pencil.

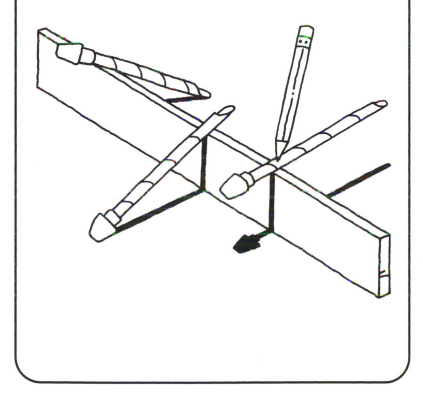

PAPER CAPERS

Charm a paper snake, electrify an ordinary newspaper, step through an index card, and defy gravity.

ABOUT PAPER

Paper is believed to have been invented by Ts'ai Lun almost two thousand years ago in China.

Chinese paper was a mixture of rags and plant fiber.

The craft of papermaking didn't spread to Europe until twelve hundred years later. Until 1700, paper was made from cotton and linen fibers.

Paper was made by hand, one sheet at a time. In 1798, Nicholas Robert of France invented the first machine to make paper, which he sold to Henry and Sealy Fourdrinier of England. Papermaking machines are still known as Fourdriniers.

Now paper is thin, flat sheets usually made from wood pulp.

The many types of paper include stationery, wax paper, cardboard, contact paper, oaktag, news-paper, wallpaper, index cards, boxes, and wrapping paper.

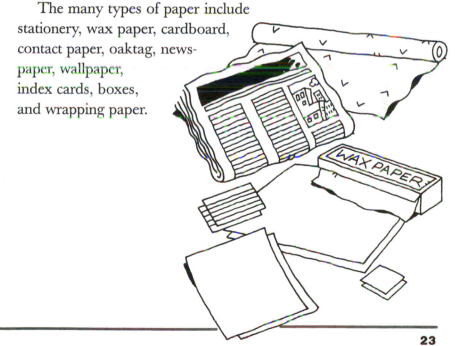

Shaping Up

Which of these shapes do you think is the strongest? No matter what materials you are working with, you can make a structure stronger by simply changing its shape.

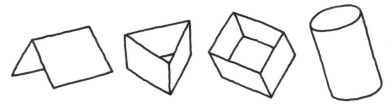

You need:

4 sheets of writing paper
a can

transparent tape
books

WHAT TO DO:

Fold the sheets of paper into various shapes, such as those shown in the illustrations.

1. Fold a sheet in half and stand it on its edges.

2. Fold a sheet in thirds and tape the ends together.

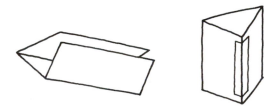

3. Fold a sheet in half lengthwise, cut on the fold, and tape the two halves together at the top and bottom. Then fold the attached halves in half again from top to bottom. Spread the sheets to form the cube.

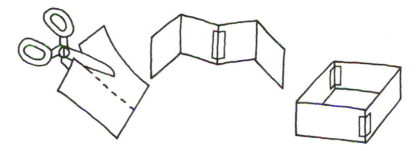

4. Roll a sheet of paper around a can, secure the paper with tape, and remove the can.

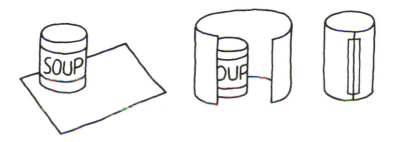

Set a light book on top of each shape. Some will collapse immediately. Keep piling books on the others until they collapse.

WHAT HAPPENS:

The round paper pillar holds a surprising number of books.

WHY:

A hollow tube is the strongest because the weight is distributed evenly over it.

Corrugated Paper

What makes a corrugated box strong?

You need:

3 sheets of typing paper

1 jar or glass

WHAT TO DO:

Make a crease about $1/4$ inch ($1/2$ cm) from the edge of one sheet of paper, fold it down, and press down on the fold. Using the first fold as a guide, fold a second crease back. Alternate folding back and forth until the entire sheet is pleated, as in the illustration.

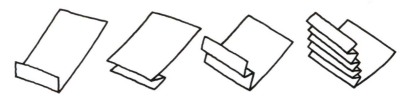

Roll the second sheet of paper around a can and tape the ends together. Remove the can. Do the same thing with the third. Line up the two paper tubes 4 inches (10 cm) apart on a table. Then place the pleated sheet on them. Rest the jar on top of the pleated sheet.

WHAT HAPPENS:

The pleated paper holds the jar.

WHY:

You have added strength by using corrugated paper, which you created by folding the sheet back and forth. An engineer devised this way of making paper stiffer—and stronger.

Powerful Paper

Just how strong can paper get?

You need:

a corrugated carton

scissors

a small board (a cutting board will do)

a quart-size (1 liter) fruit juice can

rubber bands or tape

WHAT TO DO:

Cut a strip about 4 inches by 12 inches (10 x 30 cm) from a corrugated box. Wrap the strip around the can and secure it with rubber bands or masking tape. Then remove the can.

Place a small board on top of the cardboard circle. Stand on it.

WHAT HAPPENS:

The cardboard circle will hold your weight.

WHY:

That strength comes from the combination of circular shape and corrugated paper.

Tough Newspaper

Your strongest blow cannot budge this fearless newspaper!

You need:
a newspaper
a table
a wooden ruler or a thin piece of scrap wood

WHAT TO DO:

Place the ruler on a table so that an inch or two (3–5 cm) projects over the edge. Spread a double sheet of newspaper over the ruler so that the paper lies flat along the table edge. Strike the projecting edge of the ruler as hard as you can.

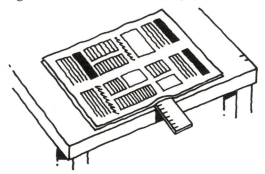

WHAT HAPPENS:

The newspaper doesn't budge.

WHY:

It is air pressure on the paper that prevents it from moving. Air pushes down with almost 15 pounds of pressure on every square inch of surface (1 kg per square centimeter). For an average sheet of newspaper, the total resistance is about 2 tons (1,800 kg).

Invisible Shield

If you've ever been caught in the rain on your way home and tried to keep dry by putting a newspaper over your head, you know that water doesn't treat paper very well. But in the following experiment, the paper seems to be protected by an invisible shield.

You need:
a sheet of newspaper
a pot of water
a glass jar

WHAT TO DO:
Crumple the sheet of newspaper and stuff it into the empty glass or jar tightly enough so that it doesn't fall out when you turn the glass upside down. Holding the glass bottom up, sink it deep into a pot filled with water. Hold it there. After a minute or so, pull the glass out of the water and remove the paper.

WHAT HAPPENS:
The paper is dry.

WHY:
Water cannot get into the glass because the "empty" glass is already filled with air. And the air cannot get out because it is lighter than water.

Why No Flood?

Until you learn how to work this experiment perfectly (and maybe even then), it's best to do it over a sink or basin.

You need:
a piece of cardboard
    or a large index card
a glass of water

WHAT TO DO:
Place the cardboard over a drinking glass filled to the brim with water.

Make sure no air bubbles enter the glass as you hold the cardboard against it. Then turn the glass upside down over a sink or basin. Take away the hand holding the cardboard.

WHAT HAPPENS:
The cardboard stays in place—and the water stays in the glass.

WHY:
The pressure of the air outside the glass is greater than the pressure of the water inside. It is the air pressure that keeps the water in the glass.

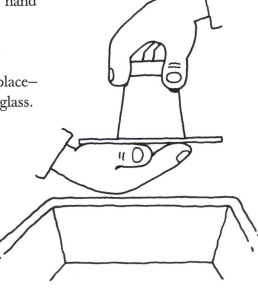

The Paper Napkin Trick

It's a good idea to practice this trick, too, where spilled water won't do any harm.

You need:
a paper napkin
a plastic cup of water

WHAT TO DO:

Drape the napkin over the edge of a kitchen counter or table. Place the plastic cup of water on one corner of the napkin about an inch (25 mm) from the edge.

Pull the napkin quickly from under the plastic cup.

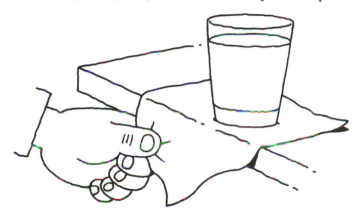

WHAT HAPPENS:

The napkin comes out—without spilling any water.

WHY:

The cup doesn't overturn because of the tendency of things at rest to stay at rest. It's that old law of motion—inertia—at work. (If it does spill, you're not pulling the napkin fast enough or with enough force.)

Cantilever Bridge

Cantilever bridges are built with two beams that project toward each other to join and form a span. How do they stay up?

You need:

5 or 6 notebooks or thin books
table

WHAT TO DO:

Stack the notebooks on the edge of a table. Slide the top one halfway out from the stack and over the table's edge. When it balances, slide it back a little. Move out the next notebook along with the top one until they balance, and then slide them back a little. Add another notebook and move the top three out and slide them back a little after they balance. Continue in the same way until all the notebooks are staggered.

WHAT HAPPENS:

The top notebook seems to be suspended in air, but the notebooks do not fall.

WHY:

You have found the center of gravity, the points at which all the weight of an object seems to be concentrated. Though the top book appears to be suspended in air, more than half the weight of the stack of notebooks is resting on the table.

Flash!

Your friends may get a charge out of this.

You need:

a sheet of newspaper
the metal top of a large can
a small piece of plastic wrap
   or wool

a friend

WHAT TO DO:

Rub a dry sheet of newspaper vigorously with the plastic wrap or wool for thirty seconds or so. Then place the top of the can in the center of the newspaper. Holding the newspaper by its edges, lift it while your friend puts a finger near the metal.

WHAT HAPPENS:

A spark!

WHY:

When an electrical charge passes between two objects, the result is a spark. As you rubbed the newspaper, you charged it with static electricity. Your friend's touch made the electrical charge jump from the paper to the uncharged can lid.

You may have seen a similar spark when you rubbed your shoes on a rug and then touched a doorknob. Or you may have heard a crackling sound while combing your hair. These are all examples of static electricity.

Lightning is a huge electric spark that results when charges jump from one cloud to another or from a cloud down to the ground.

Charming a Paper Snake

It's easier than you think to charm a snake.

You need:

thin cardboard or heavy paper	a lamp
scissors	a pencil
	string

WHAT TO DO:

Draw a spiral snake (as in the illustration) on thin cardboard or any slightly heavy paper, such as oaktag, wrapping paper, or even a large index card.

Cut out the spiral snake and tie a string to its "tail."

Suspend the snake over a lit bulb or a heated radiator.

WHAT HAPPENS:

The snake dances.

WHY:

Hot air is less dense than cold air, and therefore it rises. The moving air spins the spiral snake.

To make a stand for your snake: With a pin, attach the head to the eraser end of a pencil, letting it curl around the pencil. Stand the pencil in the center hole of a spool of thread.

Dancing Dolls

Never thought you'd see paper dolls dance?

You need:

a piece of stiff paper
  such as oaktag
a large sheet of cardboard

scissors
paste or tape
2 paper clips

a magnet
a pencil

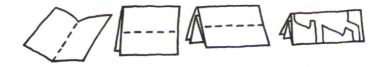

WHAT TO DO:

Fold the stiff paper from top to bottom twice. Draw the right half of a doll along the exposed top fold, extending the doll's arm and leg to the bottom of the exposed fold, as in the illustration.

Cut along the lines you drew without opening up the folded paper. Form a circle of dolls by pasting the two ends of the group together. Attach the paper clips so that the dolls stand on them.

Balance the large sheet of cardboard so that a portion of it hangs over the edge of a table. Stand the circle of paper dolls on top of the cardboard so that one of the clips is on the overhanging portion.

Move your magnet underneath the cardboard—first to the right and then to the left.

WHAT HAPPENS:

The paper dolls dance.

WHY:

The paper clips are made of steel. Therefore, the magnet attracts them—even through cardboard.

Paper Magic: The Möbius Strip

You can cause paper to have only one side! This surprising phenomenon was first discovered by a nineteenth-century German mathematician, August Ferdinand Möbius.

You need:

a sheet of paper   a pencil

scissors   tape or glue

WHAT TO DO:

Cut a strip of paper 1 inch by 10 inches (2.5 x 25 cm). Give one end a half twist and tape or glue the ends together to form a loop.

Draw a lengthwise line down the center of the strip until you reach your starting point.

Cut along the line you have drawn.

WHAT HAPPENS:

There is no side without a line!

And you wind up with only one loop—twice as long as your original loop.

WHY:

No one has been able to explain this strange "trick." But it has actually been put to practical use. Ordinarily fan belts and factory conveyor belts wear out faster on the inside than the outside. But belts made with a half twist like this wear out more evenly and more slowly.

Through the Index Card

Alice stepped through a magic looking glass—which seemed impossible. You can do the "impossible," too—stretch a very ordinary index card and step through it!

You need:
a large index card (or a piece of typing paper)
scissors

WHAT TO DO:

Fold the card or paper down the middle from top to bottom. Cut a box out along the fold. Then make seven or nine deep cuts (any odd number will do) alternating with one cut starting at the fold and the other starting at the edge of the card. Unfold the index card and stretch it out.

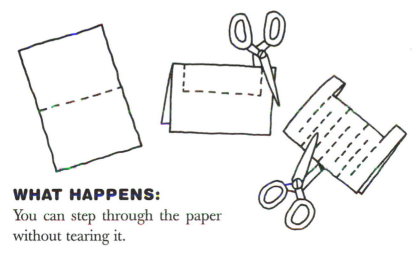

WHAT HAPPENS:

You can step through the paper without tearing it.

WHY:

Because of the way you cut the card, you stretch it first from one side and then from the other. In each case, the opposite side holds firm.

Color Fun

Is green really green?

You need:

a strip of paper towel or newspaper

a green felt-tipped pen
  or a drop of green food dye

a jar or glass with 1 inch (2.5 cm) of water

WHAT TO DO:

Make a spot of color about 2 inches (5 cm) from one end of the strip of paper towel. Hang the strip in the jar so that the spot is above the water and the end of the strip is in the water. Let it stand for fifteen to twenty minutes.

WHAT HAPPENS:

The green spot is gone—but above the original spot the paper has turned blue, and above that the paper is yellow.

WHY:

Most dyes and inks are combinations of coloring substances that can be taken apart by adding water or alcohol. Water moves up the paper in the same way that sap rises in trees. As the water moves up, it dissolves the green spot and gradually moves the color up the strip of paper. But since the colors that make up green—blue and yellow—do not move at the same rate, they separate.

Magic Colors

Mix colors the easy way!

You need:
cardboard or a paper plate
scissors
watercolors or poster paints
string or thread

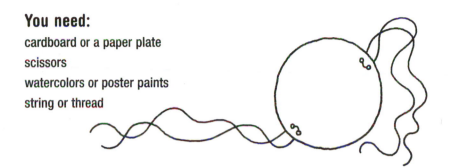

WHAT TO DO:

Cut out a circle. Color one side red and the other blue. Punch small holes on opposite sides of the disk, as in the illustration, and thread short lengths of string through each hole.

Hold the cardboard by its strings and twirl it around.

WHAT HAPPENS:

The color you see is purple.

WHY:

The eye continues to see each color for a while after it has disappeared, and so your eye and your brain mix the colors of the rapidly whirling disk.

What happens if you make one side red and the other yellow?

Benham Disk

The hand is quicker than the eye. Well, is it really? Is it magic, illusion, or trickery?

You need:
a cardboard disk
white paper
scissors
a black pen or marker
a screw with a nut (or a pin attached to the eraser of a pencil)

WHAT TO DO:

Cut a circle 4 to 5 inches (10–12 cm) in diameter out of white paper. Color one half black. Divide the white half into four equal parts. In each segment draw three black arcs about $1/4$ inch ($1/2$ cm) thick, as in the illustration.

Cut out a cardboard circle of about the same size.

Place the sheet of paper on the cardboard disk.

Mount the two on a pin attached to a pencil eraser, or push a screw through the center and secure it with a nut.

Spin the cardboard disk at various speeds, clockwise and counterclockwise.

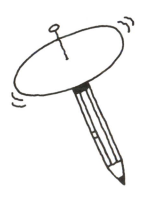

WHAT HAPPENS:

The arcs seem to close up to form six rings.

At a slow speed, spinning clockwise, the outer rings look blue and inner rings look red. When you spin them counterclockwise, the colors reverse.

WHY:

The arcs seem to close to form rings, because the eye continues to see each arc for a short time after it has disappeared.

Why do we see red and blue when the only colors on the disk are black and white? The entire color spectrum is present in white light, but our eyes register the different colors at different lengths of time.

When we spin the disk, light from the colors that make up white reach the eye but are visible for only an instant before being followed by the black portions of the disk. Our eye is only able to register a part of that color spectrum—the blue, which has the shortest rays, and the red, which has the longest.

Try varying the patterns of the white half of your Benham disk and see what interesting results you get.

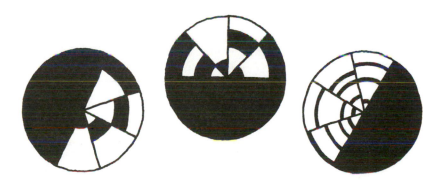

MORE THAN LEMONADE

With a little ingenuity, you can turn an ordinary lemon into invisible ink, cleaning fluid, a rock tester, a rocket launcher, and a wet cell.

ABOUT LEMONS

The lemon probably came to us from India.

The small thorny-branched lemon tree was first planted in the United States during the California Gold Rush of 1849 to fight scurvy among the prospectors.

Lemon juice is a remedy for rust, ink, and mildew stains. Oil from the lemon peel is used to make flavor extract, perfumes, cosmetics, and furniture polish.

Lemon juice is the main source of citric acid used in textile printing to keep the fabric clear of rust stains from the machinery.

Invisible Ink

You can use a lemon to write a secret message.

You need:

the juice of half a lemon

a cotton swab (or a toothpick
  wrapped in absorbent cotton,
  or a dried-up pen)

a lamp

paper

WHAT TO DO:

Dissolve the lemon juice in water and dip the swab into it. Then use the swab to write a message on ordinary white paper. When it dries, the writing will be invisible. When you want to read the message, heat the paper by holding it near a lightbulb.

WHAT HAPPENS:

The words appear on the page in black.

WHY:

The juices of lemons and other fruits contain compounds of carbon. The compounds are nearly colorless when you dissolve them in water. But when you heat them, the carbon compounds break down and produce carbon, which is black.

Lemon Cleaning Fluid

Write an invisible message with flour and water and make it appear with iodine. Then use lemon to make it disappear again.

You need:

a few drops of lemon juice
1 tablespoon (15 mL) flour
1/4 cup (60 mL) water
cotton swabs
a paper towel
a few drops of iodine

WHAT TO DO:

Mix the water with the flour. Write your message on the paper towel with a swab. When the message dries, it will be invisible.

When you are ready to read it, use a swab to apply a few drops of iodine. Your message will appear in blue-black.

Next, dab on a few drops of lemon.

WHAT HAPPENS:

Your message disappears.

Don't taste. Iodine is poisonous.

WHY:

The iodine reacts with the flour, a starch, to form a new compound that appears as blue-black.

When you apply the lemon juice, the ascorbic acid (vitamin C) of the lemon combines with the iodine to make a new colorless compound. So if you spill iodine on anything, you can use lemon juice to remove it. It also removes ink, mildew, and rust stains from paper and cloth.

Bright as a Penny

Soap and water won't clean metals very easily. That takes a special cleaner—or you can try lemon or vinegar!

You need:
2 tablespoons (30 mL) lemon juice or vinegar

a dull penny or other copper coin

a small glass or paper cup

WHAT TO DO:
Soak the coin in lemon juice for five minutes.

WHAT HAPPENS:
You fish out a shiny coin!

WHY:
Oxygen in the air combined with the copper to form the dull copper oxide coating. The acid of the lemon acts chemically to remove the oxide. The results? A bright copper penny.

Nifty Nail

Dig out that pile of pennies you've been saving and make yourself a copper-plated nail.

You need:

1/4 to 1/2 cup (60–120 mL) lemon juice or vinegar	large, clean nail
	salt
10 to 20 dull copper pennies	small glass or jar

WHAT TO DO:

Put the pennies into a glass and cover them with lemon juice or vinegar. Add a pinch of salt. Let them stand for two or three minutes.

Clean the nail with scouring powder and water. Then add the nail to the solution.

Wait at least fifteen minutes. Then fish out the nail.

WHAT HAPPENS:

The nail is coated with copper.

WHY:

Copper from the pennies interacts with the acid of the lemon juice to form a new compound (copper citrate). When you insert the nail into the solution, the compound plates the nail with a thin layer of copper that cannot be rubbed off.

Once you've got your copper nail, you might want to wear it on a string.

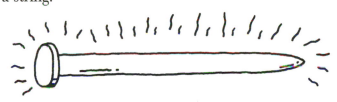

Save That Apple!

Lemon can also keep apple pie fresh.

You need:
1 lemon
1 apple

WHAT TO DO:
Cut the apple into four parts. Squeeze lemon juice on two of them. Let all the apple pieces stand for several hours.

WHAT HAPPENS:
The pieces of apple that were not treated with lemon turn brown. The apple pieces that were doctored with lemon juice do not.

WHY:
When exposed to air, certain chemicals in the apple react by destroying cells, which turn brown. But the vitamin C (ascorbic acid) in the lemon slows down the reaction between the chemicals in the fruit and the oxygen in the air. This preserves the color and taste of the apple.

How to Make Red Cabbage "Litmus" Paper

You need:
a jar of red cabbage or a small head of fresh red cabbage

a wide-mouthed jar

paper towels

WHAT TO DO:
Use the liquid from a jar of red cabbage, or make your own by grating part of a fresh red cabbage and boiling it for ten minutes or more. Let the red cabbage juice cool and then strain it into a wide-mouthed jar.

Soak 2-inch (5 cm) strips of paper towel in the cabbage juice for a minute and let them dry. Your "litmus" paper is now ready for testing. It will turn red-pink in acid and green in alkali. You can also experiment and make indicators from fruits, flowers, other vegetables, and even tea. The color change will be different, though.

The litmus paper used in schools and in chemical labs is colored by lichens, plants that are combinations of algae and fungi.

Lemon Lifesaver

Poison control centers used to recommend vinegar or lemon juice as an antidote for some poisons. This experiment shows why. You will need litmus paper, but that's no problem—you can use the liquid of red cabbage to make your own (see box on page 49).

You need:
a few drops of lemon juice or vinegar
red cabbage "litmus" paper
a few drops of ammonia
latex or rubber gloves

WHAT TO DO:

Apply a few drops of lemon to one strip of "litmus" paper. Add a few drops of ammonia to a second strip. *(Be very careful when handling the ammonia. Protect your skin from irritation by putting on latex or rubber gloves beforehand.)* Then apply a few drops of lemon to the spot made by the ammonia.

WHAT HAPPENS:

The strip with lemon juice on it turns pink. The strip with ammonia added turns green. When you add lemon to the green ammonia spot, it returns to its original reddish purple color.

WHY:

The pink color indicates the presence of acid because lemon is a mild acid, a nonmetal combined with hydrogen.

The green color indicates the presence of alkali because ammonia is an alkali (otherwise known as a base), a metal combined with hydroxide. The "litmus" paper returns to its original color when the ammonia is acted against–neutralized–by the lemon, its chemical opposite.

What does all this have to do with poison? Ammonia is poisonous if someone drinks it. Since lemon neutralizes ammonia, it was once recommended as a temporary antidote, just enough to last until you could get to a doctor. The current emergency treatment for accidentally drinking a poison such as ammonia is to dilute it by drinking large amounts of water or milk.

Acid or Base

Use your red cabbage indicator to determine which foods are acids and which are bases (alkali).

You need:

5–10 tablespoons (75–150 mL) of red cabbage juice

5–10 small glasses or paper cups

WHAT TO DO:

Put a tablespoon of red cabbage juice in each glass or cup. Add lemon juice to one, grapefruit juice to the second, tomato or pineapple juice to a third, vinegar to the fourth. Then test baking soda, milk, rubbing alcohol, oil, soap, and other household products.

Those that turn pink are acids. Those that turn green are bases.

Blowing Up a Balloon with a Lemon

Put chemistry to work for you!

You need:
juice of 1 lemon or 1/4 cup (60 mL) vinegar
a balloon
an empty soda bottle
2 tablespoons (30 mL) water
1 teaspoon (5 mL) baking soda

WHAT TO DO:
Stretch the balloon to make the rubber easier to inflate. Dissolve the baking soda in the water in the clean, empty soda bottle, then stir in the lemon juice or vinegar. Quickly fit the stretched balloon over the mouth of the bottle.

WHAT HAPPENS:
The balloon inflates.

WHY:
When you mix the base (the baking soda) and the acid (the lemon or vinegar), you create carbon dioxide, a gas that rises into the balloon and blows it up.

Rock Tester

How do geologists identify their specimens? This is one way.

You need:

a small sampling of various rocks, including limestone or marble

1/4 cup (60 mL) lemon juice or vinegar

WHAT TO DO:

Pour the lemon juice or vinegar over the rock.

WHAT HAPPENS:

The liquid bubbles on some but not on others.

WHY:

When the lemon juice bubbles, the rock sample is either limestone or marble. Limestone, a sedimentary rock formed under water from mud and silt, contains a carbonate form of calcium, an alkaline earth metal. When you add the lemon (an acid) to the alkaline limestone, it forms carbon dioxide. That makes the liquid bubble up, just as pancakes and cakes puff up when you add baking soda to the batter. Actually, baking soda can be made from limestone. Marble is a rock formed under great heat and pressure from limestone. It reacts to acid just as limestone does.

You get similar results if you add lemon juice to chalk, because it too is made of limestone.

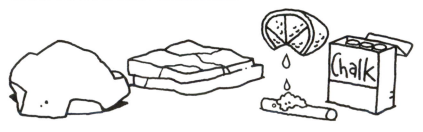

Make Your Own Lemon Soda

You can make a bubbly lemon or orange soda that is tasty enough to drink.

You need:

a lemon or orange

1 teaspoon (5 mL) baking soda

a large glass

sugar or some other sweetener (to taste)

water

WHAT TO DO:

Squeeze the juice from a lemon or orange and add an equal amount of water. Stir in the baking soda. Taste and add sugar if you like.

WHAT HAPPENS:

The liquid will be bubbly and taste like lemon or orange soda.

WHY:

The bubbles are carbon dioxide gas formed when you combine the base (the baking soda) with the acid (the lemon or orange juice).

The bubbles in real soda are also created by carbon dioxide, added under pressure to water, flavor, and sweetener.

Lemon Rocket

Launch a rocket by following instructions exactly. You don't want the rocket to go off before you're out of the way!

You need:

empty soda bottle with cork to fit

1/4 cup (60 mL) lemon juice or vinegar

1 teaspoon (5 mL) baking soda

a square of paper towel

2 paper towel strips, 1 inch by 10 inches (2.5 cm x 25 cm)

water

tacks or tape

WHAT TO DO:

Fit a cork to a soda bottle, trimming it or padding it with part of the square of paper towel if necessary. Tack or tape the two paper towel strips to the cork. Put the cork aside; it will be your rocket.

Pour a mixture of water and lemon juice into the soda bottle until it is half-filled. Wrap the baking soda in a little square of paper towel.

Go outside where your rocket has plenty of space to travel. Then drop the wrapped-up baking soda into the bottle and insert the cork loosely. Put the bottle on the ground and stand back.

WHAT HAPPENS:

The cork will eventually shoot up.

WHY:

As the water and lemon juice soak through the paper towel, the baking soda reacts to produce carbon dioxide. As more gas forms, pressure builds up inside the bottle and sends the cork flying.

Shock Them All!

Want to shock your friends? You can do it by repeating an experiment first done by the Italian physicist Alessandro Volta two hundred years ago.

You need:

lemon juice

9 1-inch-by-1-inch (2.5 cm x 2.5 cm) squares of paper towel

5 pennies or other copper coins

5 dimes (or any other coin that is not copper)

WHAT TO DO:

Soak the paper towel squares in the lemon juice. Make a pile of coins, alternating dimes and pennies. Separate each one with a lemon-soaked strip of paper towel.

Moisten the tip of one finger on each hand and hold the pile between your fingers.

WHAT HAPPENS:

You get a small shock or tingle.

WHY:

You have made a wet cell, the forerunner of the battery we buy at the hardware store. The lemon juice, an acid solution, conducts the electricity created by the separated metals of the two coins.

What we call a battery is actually two or more dry cells. In each dry cell, two metals (a zinc metal container and a carbon rod) are separated by blotting paper soaked in a strong acid.

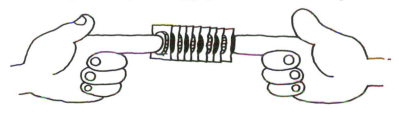

Turn That Lemon On

You can make electricity with your lemon!

You need:

a lemon
a galvanometer (see page 60 for how to make your own)
2 stiff copper wires
large paper clip
scissors

WHAT TO DO:

If there is any insulation on the ends of the wire, strip it off. Untwist the paper clip and attach it to an end of one of the wires. Squeeze and roll the lemon to loosen the pulp inside. Make two small cuts in the skin of the lemon an inch (2.5 cm) or so apart. Insert the bare wire and the paper clip through the skin of the lemon and into the juicy part. The two wires should be close to each other but not touching.

Connect the free ends of the two wires to the terminals of the meter (or to the free ends of the wires of the homemade galvanometer).

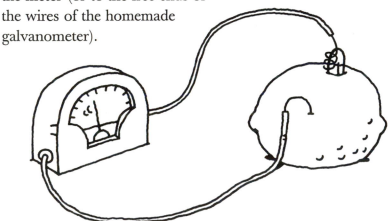

WHAT HAPPENS:

The meter moves.

WHY:

Chemical reactions of the two different metals (the copper of the wire and the iron of the clip) in the acid (lemon juice) draw electrons away from one wire toward the other. They flow out of the lemon through one wire, go through the meter, and then enter the lemon by the other wire.

If your hardware or electrical supply store can provide a bulb of less than 1.5 volts, try connecting several lemons and see how many lemon wet cells it will take to light the bulb. Line up the lemons so that you can link them to one another, with a bare copper wire and a clip in each, as in the illustration. You should wind up with two free wire ends, one attached to a clip. Connect these wire ends to the bulb.

Making a Galvanometer

A galvanometer is an instrument designed to detect electric currents. You can make one with a few simple materials.

You need:

a compass (or make one; see page 61)

15 feet (4.5 m) of bell wire (from the hardware store)

small rectangular cardboard box

WHAT TO DO:

Place the compass in the center of a small cardboard box. Scrape off about $1/2$ inch (1 cm) of insulation from each end of the bell wire. Starting about 6 inches (15 cm) from one end, wind the wire tightly around the box, circling it about two dozen times. Leave another 6 inches (15 cm) of wire free on the other side of the box.

Rest your galvanometer on the table so that it is horizontal and turn it until the compass needle is parallel to the coil of wire.

Attach the bell wire ends to the wires of the lemon cell.

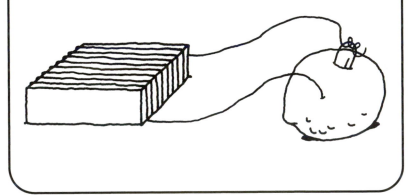

How to Make a Compass

You need:

a needle

a magnet

a dish of water

a cork 1/4 to 1/2 inch (1/2–1 cm) thick

WHAT TO DO:

Magnetize the needle by stroking it at least fifty times in one direction with either pole of the magnet. Float the cork in the dish of water. Carefully center the needle on the cork.

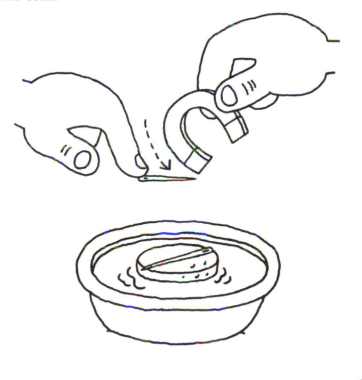

A Taste of Electricity

If you touch the two wires that you've inserted in the lemon to your tongue at the same time, you will taste something metallic and feel a slight tingling sensation. You are tasting and feeling electricity!

Baby Lemons

Don't throw out those lemon seeds. Plant them, and eventually you may have a lemon tree! At the very least, you can get them to sprout.

You need:

seeds of several lemons
water
blotter paper or paper towels

a wide-mouthed jar or glass
bits of paper towel
or absorbent cotton

WHAT TO DO:

Soak the seeds overnight in water to soften the outside layer.

Wet a piece of blotter paper or paper towel and line a jar or glass with it. Fill the center of the glass with the bits of paper towel or cotton. Near the top of the jar, push the seeds between the outside of the jar and the towel bits or cotton. Pour an inch (2.5 cm) or so of water in the bottom of the glass, and add more as it gets absorbed. Place it in a warm, dark place like a closet or cabinet.

WHAT HAPPENS:

In a week or ten days, the seeds will begin to sprout.

WHY:

Seeds contain "baby plants" or embryos. The embryos in the seeds may grow into new plants if you give them moisture and warm air. The blotter supplies the moisture without waterlogging them.

Lemon Penicillin

Grow your own microbes with a lemon, water, darkness—and patience.

You need:
a lemon
water
plastic wrap or aluminum foil
a clean empty container
a magnifying glass or hand lens

WHAT TO DO:

Place a lemon in an empty clean container. Add a few drops of water and cover the container tightly with plastic wrap or aluminum foil. Store it for a week or more in a dark place, such as a kitchen cabinet.

Then take out the lemon. Look at it carefully with a magnifying glass.

WHAT HAPPENS:

You will see soft, green mold growing on the lemon. (Don't touch the mold or breathe it because you may be allergic to it.)

WHY:

The green fuzzy mold on the lemons is actually a colony of millions of one-celled plants growing together. They grow on food that is kept too long and make it change color and smell bad.

This particular mold, the same kind that grows on blue cheese, is the one from which scientists make penicillin, the medicine that fights harmful microbes when we're sick.

When you finish examining it, place the moldy lemon in the container and replace the wrapping. Dump it in the nearest trash can—and wash your hands.

Ripe Fruit in a Hurry

Try putting that moldy lemon in a paper bag with some unripe pears or peaches and note the results. The green mold on the lemon gives off a gas called ethylene. The mold gives off so much gas that a single moldy lemon can speed up the ripening of hundreds of pieces of unripe fruit.

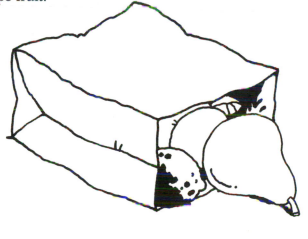

DAIRY DOZEN

The refrigerator can supply the raw materials for many fascinating—and useful—experiments. You can construct a plastic toy, etch graffiti on an eggshell, and make a "fat" light meter.

ABOUT MILK
Mammals, including people, feed their young with milk from the mother's body. Most of our milk comes from cows, but humans also use the milk of the horse, goat, sheep, buffalo, camel, donkey, zebra, reindeer, llama, and yak.

ABOUT BUTTER
Butter—probably from buffalo—was known by 2000 BC. First used as an ointment to beautify hair, it was also used as a medicine to treat burns, and as oil for lamps.

People make butter by churning or agitating milk or cream and separating the solid fatty portion.

ABOUT OIL
Our word **oil** comes from the Greek for "olive," but we use many different kinds of oil from animals and from plants such as cottonseed, palm, corn, peanut, and soybean.

ABOUT EGGS
Various wild birds were first tamed for use as food—flesh and eggs—in India.

Making Muffet Food

Little Miss Muffet was eating her curds and whey when that spider came along. Just what are curds and whey?

You need:
1 cup (240 mL) milk
1/3 cup (80 mL) vinegar
a wide-mouthed jar

WHAT TO DO:
In the jar, mix the milk and vinegar.

WHAT HAPPENS:
The milk changes. At the bottom is a thick substance (the curds) and on top is a watery liquid (the whey).

WHY:
Vinegar turns the milk sour and separates some of its parts. Curds are made up of the fat and minerals and a protein called casein. Cheese is made from curds. White glue is made from the casein of the curds. To use the curds as glue, just wash away the liquid.

Make a Plastic Toy

HOT!

Create your own plastic and mold it into a tiny toy. Don't expect it to look store-bought!

You need:
1/2 cup (120 mL) milk
1 teaspoon (5 mL) vinegar
a small pan
a small clean jar

WHAT TO DO:
Heat the milk in the pan until it forms lumps (curdles). Slowly pour off the liquid. Put the lumps into the jar and add the vinegar. Let stand for an hour or so.

WHAT HAPPENS:
A rubbery blob forms. Again slowly pour off the liquid and shape the blob into a ball or a face. Leave it to harden for a few hours or longer in the open jar or on a paper towel. Color it with acrylic paints if you wish.

WHY:
When the vinegar and milk interact, the milk separates into a liquid and a solid made of fat, minerals, and the protein casein (made up of very long molecules that bend like rubber until they harden).

At first, plastics were made from milk and plants. Now they are made from petroleum, and this poses a problem, because petroleum-based plastics don't decompose.

Detecting the Hard-Boiled Egg

What a dilemma! You put a cooked egg in the refrigerator, and someone stuck it back among the raw eggs. You need the cooked one for a salad. But which one is it?

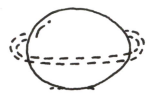

WHAT TO DO:
Spin each egg. Note what happens. Then touch each spinning egg lightly.

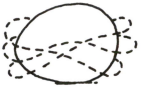

WHAT HAPPENS:
Most of the eggs wobble, but one spins. The spinner is the hard-boiled egg. When you touch the spinning hard-boiled egg lightly, it stops spinning completely. The raw eggs move again after you've tried to stop them.

WHY:
The loose yolks and white in the raw eggs revolve slowly because of inertia, the tendency of an object to continue at rest or in motion. This causes the raw eggs to wobble and to continue to move even after you try to stop them. The solid white and yolk cause the hard-boiled egg to respond more quickly.

How Do You Make an Egg Float?

No, this is not a riddle! Find out why it's easier to swim in the ocean than in a freshwater lake or pool!

You need:

an egg

a glass of water

12 tablespoons (180 mL) or more of salt

WHAT TO DO:

1. Put an egg in a glass half full of water. Notice what happens. Add several tablespoons of salt, stir gently, and observe what happens.

2. To half a glass of salty water (10 tablespoons [150 mL] or more of salt), slowly add half a glass of fresh water. Don't stir. Gently lower in the egg.

WHAT HAPPENS:

1. In the fresh water the egg sinks. As you add salt, it floats higher and higher.

2. When you add fresh water to the very salty water, the egg is suspended in the middle!

WHY:

1. The denser the liquid, the greater its upward lift (or buoyancy). Salt makes the water denser.

2. When you add fresh water to the salty water, it remains on top. The egg sinks through it and floats on the lower, denser, salty water.

The Egg-in-the-Bottle Trick

Can you really put an egg into a bottle with a neck that's slightly smaller than the egg—without mashing the egg?

You need:

a hard-boiled egg, peeled

a small-necked jar, such as a ketchup bottle, baby bottle, or water jug

boiling water

WHAT TO DO:

Pour boiling water into the bottle. Shake it around and then pour it out. Quickly place the egg over the mouth of the bottle.

WHAT HAPPENS:

Even though the egg is larger than the opening, the egg drops into the bottle.

WHY:

The hot water leaves steam in the bottle, which forces out some of the air. As the steam in the bottle cools, it changes into droplets of water and requires less space. This reduces the amount of air pressure in the bottle, and so the pressure of the outside air pushes the egg inside the bottle.

To remove the egg, hold the bottle upside down, place your mouth on the opening of the bottle, and blow into it for thirty seconds. The pressure inside will be greater than outside—and so the egg will be forced out.

Egg Power

Eggshells are fragile, aren't they? Or are they?

Collect the empty eggshells when the family has scrambled eggs or omelets for breakfast.

WHAT TO DO:

Wrap a piece of masking tape around the midsection of each empty eggshell half. Then, with your scissors, trim off the excess shell so that each one has a straight-edged bottom.

Lay out the four eggshells, dome up, so that they form a square. Holding it upright, stand a can on the eggshells. Keep on stacking cans on top of that one until the shells crack.

WHAT HAPPENS:

The "fragile" eggshells can support a surprising amount of weight.

WHY:

The secret of their strength is their shape. No single point in the dome supports the entire weight of the object on top of it. The weight is carried down along the curved walls to the wide base.

Egg Graffiti

Can you etch your initials or a drawing on an ordinary egg without breaking the shell?

You need:

a hard-boiled egg   a crayon

1 cup (240 mL) vinegar   a jar

WHAT TO DO:

Carefully draw or write on the egg with the crayon. Put the egg in the jar, cover it with the vinegar, and let it stand for several hours. Then dump out the vinegar. Replace it with fresh vinegar, and allow the egg to stand in it for another hour or two. Then wash the egg and remove the wax crayon marks.

WHAT HAPPENS:

The eggshell may be very fragile, but your drawing or writing remains!

WHY:

The acid in the vinegar combines with the calcium carbonate of the shell and dissolves much of it—but not the part that you wrote on with the wax crayon. The wax protects that part of the shell from the vinegar so that the section with your drawing is not dissolved.

Oil and Water

"They're like oil and water!" That's how we talk about two people who don't get along. Well, how do oil and water get along?

You need:

oil
narrow jar with a lid or a cork
water (colored with food coloring)

WHAT TO DO:

Put a tablespoon or two (15–30 mL) of oil and an equal amount of colored water into a narrow jar or soda bottle. Cover the jar and shake it hard.

WHAT HAPPENS:

Though the two seem to mix when you shake the jar, they separate when you put the jar down. The oil floats on top.

WHY:

Many liquids dissolve in water to form a solution, but water and oil do not mix. The oil molecules have a greater attraction for each other than for the molecules of the water. Oil floats on top of the water because it weighs less. That's why it is so easy to remove the fat from chicken soup and from beef gravy. When these liquids stand for a while, and especially after they have cooled, the fats form a solid layer on top of the other liquids.

Liquid Sandwich

Can you make a sandwich with three liquids?

You need:

2 tablespoons (30 mL) oil
2 tablespoons (30 mL) water
2 tablespoons (30 mL) honey or molasses
narrow jar with lid or cork

WHAT TO DO:

Into a narrow jar, pour the oil, water, and honey or molasses. Cover the jar.

WHAT HAPPENS:

A liquid sandwich! The honey or molasses sinks to the bottom; the oil floats on top; and the water remains in the middle.

WHY:

The honey or molasses sinks because it is denser (it weighs more for the same amount) than water. The oil floats because it is less dense than the water.

How Fat Is It?

It's surprisingly simple to find out whether a food has fat in it.

You need:

butter or margarine

peanut butter

cream or whole milk

a sheet of paper

a pencil

lemon

honey

potato chips

WHAT TO DO:

Draw six to nine small circles on the paper. Label each circle with one of the foods you will be testing. Rub a bit of each food on its own circle. After ten minutes, examine both sides of the paper.

WHAT HAPPENS:

Some of the circles will be dry. Others will be greasy and the spot will be spreading.

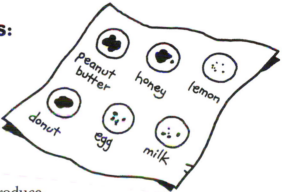

WHY:

Both water and fat produce a spot by filling in the spaces between the fibers of the paper. Spots made by water in the food evaporate in the air and dry. But the fat globules remain. They can only be broken down by soap or a solvent such as ether.

A "Fat" Light Meter

Which lightbulb is brighter? Which flashlight? Can you figure it out scientifically?

You need:

cooking oil or margarine
2 lamps with bulbs of different wattages
a ruler or tape measure
paper

WHAT TO DO:

Place a few drops of ordinary cooking oil or margarine on a sheet of white paper. Let it soak in and then blot away the excess so that all you have is an oil spot on the paper.

Working in a dark room, set up your lightbulbs in two unshaded lamps across a table from each other. Hold the paper close to the bulb on the left and gradually move it closer to the bulb on the right. Keep your eye on the oil spot.

WHAT HAPPENS:

The spot disappears when the same amount of light falls on both sides of the paper.

WHY:

How does that help us find out which bulb is brighter?

If we measure the distance from the spot to each bulb and the distances are not equal, one of the lights has to be brighter than the other.

For example, if bulb A is 2 feet (60 cm) away from the paper and bulb B is 3 feet (90 cm) away, bulb B is brighter. If you want to know how much brighter, multiply A's distance – 2 feet (60 cm)–by itself (2 x 2). Then multiply B's distance–3 feet (90 cm)–by itself (3 x 3). Divide the larger number by the smaller (9 ÷ 4). Bulb B gives off more than twice as much light as bulb A.

Magnifying Glass

A magnifying glass made out of water? Impossible?

You need:
butter or cooking oil
a paper clip or piece of wire hanger
water
a telephone directory, newspaper, or postage stamp

WHAT TO DO:

Straighten a paper clip or snip off a 4-inch (10 cm) piece of wire hanger by bending the wire back and forth a number of times. Form a small loop at one end of the wire and rub a little butter, margarine, or cooking oil on it. Dip the loop into a glass of water and lift it out. You now have a lens—a sort of frame that holds a layer of water.

Use the lens to read the small print in a telephone directory, the classified ads in a newspaper, or the fine details of a postage stamp.

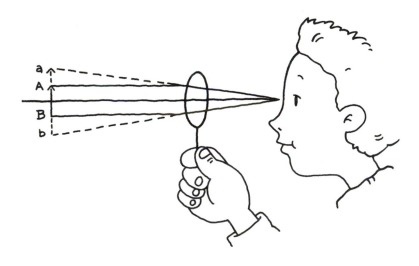

WHY:

The water lens, just like a glass or plastic lens, has a definite shape. It bends light rays as they pass through it. First, it bends light as the light enters. Then it bends it again as the light leaves. The angle at which the water bends the light depends upon the shape of the lens.

Reflected light spreads out from the object you are looking at, hits the lens, and is bent back to your eye. Your eye sees the light as though it came on a straight line from the object–and the object seems to be much larger than it actually is.

How Much Bigger?

You can find out just how much larger a lens makes an object by using a piece of graph paper. You can also use an ordinary typing sheet, but you need to draw graph lines on it like this:

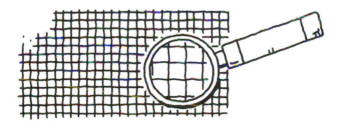

Look through your magnifying glass at the lined paper. Count the number of lines you see through the "lens" compared to the number you see outside of it.

If there are four lines outside compared to one inside, the lens magnifies four times.

ADVENTURES WITH STRING

With a piece of string, you can perform all kinds of scientific marvels! You can force water to walk a tightrope, cut a string inside a bottle, lift a heavy weight with a button, make a grandfather clock—and even prove your superior strength!

ABOUT STRING

Through the centuries, string, cord, rope, and twine have been made from the fiber of plants such as hemp, flax, jute, and sisal. Strands of the fiber are twisted or braided together. Now we also use man-made materials, like nylon and polyester.

Water Walks a Tightrope

Will water travel on a string without falling off?

You need:

a 12-inch (30 cm) string
a small nail
a pot or pail
a plastic cup
water

WHAT TO DO:

Punch a small hole near the top lip of the plastic cup with a nail or paper clip. Dampen the string and thread it through the hole, tying a knot on the inside. Fill the cup almost to the top with water.

Place a pot or pail on the floor near your left foot. Tie the free end of the string to your left index finger and hold it over the pot.

Then hold the cup up in your right hand. Stretch the string taut and slant it down toward the pot. Tip the cup of water and slowly pour the water onto the string.

WHAT HAPPENS:

The water travels down the string until it reaches your left index finger and the pot

WHY:

The molecules near the surface of the water cling together to form an elastic tubelike skin through which the water flows along the wet string. This elastic skin is known as surface tension.

Making a Figure 8 Stopper Knot

You can secure the string to the inside of the cup in any way that holds. But if you want to do it with a figure 8 stopper, follow the diagram below.

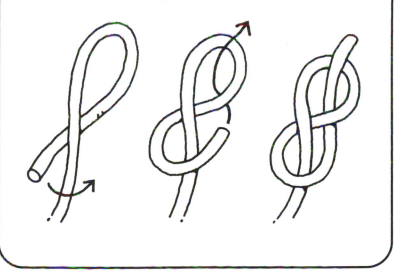

Cut a String Without Touching It

Can you cut a string without laying a hand on it—when it is inside a covered glass jar? See how easy it is when you "concentrate"!

You need:

a string   a jar with a top

tape   a magnifying glass

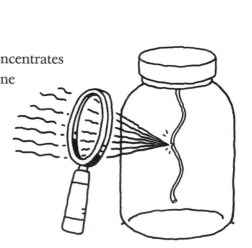

WHAT TO DO:

Suspend the string from the inside of the jar lid with tape and insert it into the jar. Screw on the jar lid.

With the magnifying glass, focus the rays of the sun on the string for a few minutes.

WHAT HAPPENS:

The string breaks in two.

WHY:

The magnifying glass concentrates the heat of the sun on one spot on the string. The heat becomes intense enough to burn right through the string.

Rescue an Ice Cube

A great icebreaker for a party! Challenge your guests to use a string to rescue an ice cube from a glass of water without getting their hands wet. Tell them they may use anything on the party table except the dishes or utensils. After they fail, show them how to do it.

You need:

a 6-inch (15 cm) piece of string or sewing thread
an ice cube
a glass of water
salt

WHAT TO DO:

Float the ice cube in the glass of water. Hang one end of the string over the edge of the glass. Place the other end of it on the ice cube. Then sprinkle a little salt on the ice cube and let it stand for five or ten minutes.

WHAT HAPPENS:

The string freezes onto the ice cube. Then you pull on the string and lift the ice cube out of the water.

WHY:

When the salt strikes the ice, it lowers the freezing point of water to a little below 32°F (0°C) and causes the surface of the ice cube to melt a little. As the ice refreezes, it traps the string.

Mining Salt

In some tropical areas, salt is not mined from the earth but taken from sea water in shallow ponds. You can create your own salt water—and then separate the salt in the form of crystals.

You need:
a piece of string
salt
tablespoon
a nail or paper clip
a small jar
hot water
a pencil

WHAT TO DO:
Fill the jar with hot water and stir in 1 tablespoon (15 mL) of salt at a time until the salt no longer dissolves. It will take about a tablespoon (15 mL) of salt for every 2 tablespoons (30 mL) of water.

Attach the nail to one end of the string. Wrap the other end of the string around a pencil. Rest the pencil on the edge of the jar and suspend the nail in the jar of salted water so that it hangs down but doesn't touch the bottom of the jar.

Place the jar in a warm place.

WHAT HAPPENS:
After a few days, the water dries up and crystals form on the string. They taste salty.

WHY:

Water molecules slowly go into the air as water vapor. As the water evaporates from the salt water, the salt atoms draw close together, forming cube-shaped crystals. When the water is gone, the salt crystals remain.

Making Rock Candy

You can make rock candy (sugar crystals) the same way you make salt crystals. Add 1 cup (240 mL) of sugar to ½ cup (120 mL) hot water, put in the string, and let it stand for a few days.

Something Fishy

Here's an easy way to spin a sea monster!

You need:

a length of string attached
   to a weight (a nail or stone)

a piece of cardboard

a pencil

scissors

a thumbtack

WHAT TO DO:

1. Draw and cut out a sea monster, like the drawing. Add three dots, one each at the top and on two sides.

2. Tack up the monster at the top dot and drop the weight from the tack. Draw along the string line. Repeat for the other two dots.

3. Tack up the monster at the point where the three lines cross. Spin it.

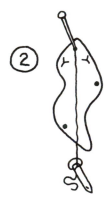

WHAT HAPPENS:

The cardboard spins evenly and stops each time at a different place.

WHY:

The point where the three lines intersect is the center of gravity. If you hang the shape by any other point, it will be out of balance, spin unevenly, and stop at the same place every time you spin it (where the center of gravity is lowest).

Getting It Straight

Bet you can't straighten this string!

You need:

a string 24 to 36 inches (60–90 cm) long
a heavy book

WHAT TO DO:

Place a heavy book in the middle of the string. Tie the string around the book without making a knot. Lift the book by holding the ends of the string. Then take an end of the string in each hand and pull on the string so that the two ends of it form one straight line.

WHAT HAPPENS:

You can't pull the string straight—no matter how hard you pull.

WHY:

You will notice that as you separate the string ends, the book feels heavier and heavier. The greater the angle between the two halves of the string, the greater the force you need to hold the book up. A straight line forms an angle of 180°. You would need an immense amount of force to hold up the book with the strings at that angle—so much that the string would break before you got the two halves to form a straight line.

Lazy Bones

You might expect the thin threads that support the stick in this experiment to break, but instead . . .

You need:
2 long pieces of thread
a thin wooden stick
a wooden hanger
a metal-edged wooden ruler

WHAT TO DO:

Tie a piece of thread to each end of the stick. Then tie the other end of each thread to the hanger so that the stick is suspended underneath. Use clove hitches if you like. (See box on p. 93.) Strike the stick with the metal edge of the ruler.

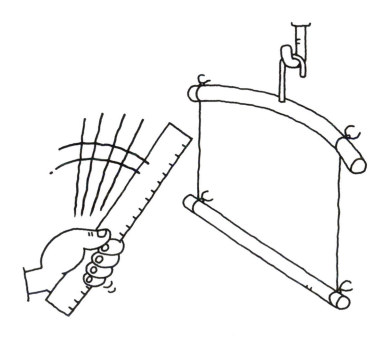

WHAT HAPPENS:

The threads do not break! If you strike hard enough, the piece of wood breaks.

WHY:

You are applying force not to the threads but to the stick. The stick resists moving—so much so that it would rather break than move. It's the law of inertia again: Bodies at rest tend to stay at rest.

Making a Clove Hitch

The clove hitch is a knot that allows you to join a rope to something else, such as a stick or a hanger.

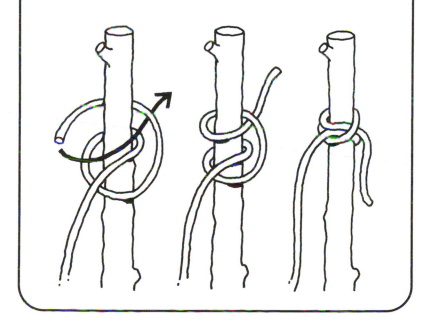

Loop-the-Loop

When you're on a loop-the-loop roller coaster and it turns upside down, why don't you fall out?

You need:

a 24-inch (60 cm)
  piece of rope

a pail

a soft rubber ball

WHAT TO DO:

Tie the rope securely to the handle of the pail. Put the ball into the pail.

Choose a spot where there's no risk of hitting anything—outdoors if possible. Hold the pail by the rope and whirl the pail in circles in the air as fast as you can.

WHAT HAPPENS:

The ball remains in the pail even when it turns upside down.

WHY:

Centrifugal force—the force created by that whirling motion—equals the force of gravity and keeps the ball from falling out of the pail. It pulls the object against the sides of the pail rather than down and out of the pail.

When you get really good at this, you may want to try it with a pail of water—outdoors!

David and Goliath

Can a button lift a stone?

You need:

a string 24 to 30 inches (60–75 cm) long

a spool (with or without thread on it)

a button

a small stone

WHAT TO DO:

Thread the string through the spool so that about two-thirds of the string is above the spool. Then tie the button to one end of the string and the stone to the other. With the button toward the top and the stone toward the bottom, hold the contraption above your head. To do this, hold the spool with one hand and, with the other hand, hold the string just above the stone. Start whirling the spool around so that both weights move as fast as possible.

Gradually let go of the string below the spool.

WHAT HAPPENS:

The heavy weight seems to be lifted up by the small one.

WHY:

Of course, the button isn't doing the lifting! When you whirl the weights fast enough, centrifugal force—the force created by the whirling motion—is greater than the force of gravity. And so the stone moves up, against the pull of gravity.

The Talking String

Make your string talk!

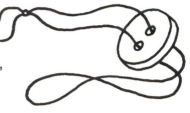

You need:
18 to 24 inches (45–60 cm) of strong,
  thin string or thread

a large 2-hole button

WHAT TO DO:
Thread the string through the holes of the button and knot the ends together. Use a bowline (see p. 97) if you like. Center the button.

Loop the string on each side of the button on your index fingers. Swing the button around a number of times, either toward or away from you, but always in the same direction.

Once the string is wound up, separate your hands, pulling the string taut. Then bring your hands together, releasing it. Alternate pulling and releasing until the string unwinds.

WHAT HAPPENS:
The button spins very fast until it twists in the opposite direction. If you spin fast enough, you hear a whirring sound.

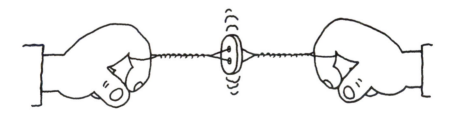

WHY:

The law of inertia—a body in motion tends to continue in motion—is at work again! The sound comes from the vibration of the air around the string.

Making a Bowline

You can tie the string to itself with a bowline, as shown in the illustration below.

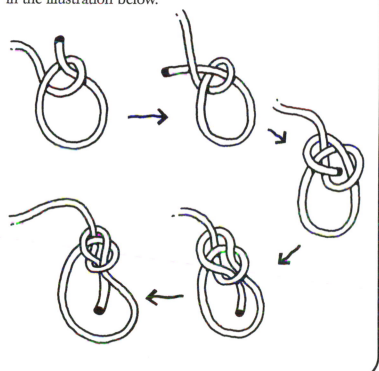

Broomstick Block-and-Tackle

You are amazingly strong! To prove it . . .

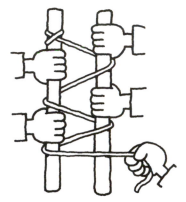

You need:
a jump rope or clothesline
2 brooms or long sticks
2 friends

WHAT TO DO:

Give a broomstick to each of your friends and ask them to stand a few feet apart. Then tie one end of the rope to one of the sticks and weave the ropes in and around the sticks, as in the illustration. You hold on to the other end of the rope. Now ask your friends to pull the broomsticks apart as hard as they can while you pull on the rope.

WHAT HAPPENS:

No matter how hard your friends try to keep them apart, you can pull the broomsticks together.

WHY:

Each time you wrap the rope around the broomsticks, you increase the distance the rope has to be pulled. When you pull on the end of the rope, you exert a small force—but over a long distance. The resulting force is far greater than the force your friends can exert over a shorter distance.

The broomstick block-and-tackle is a form of double pulley. It is used for loading ships, lifting the shovels of cranes, and lowering and lifting lifeboats, pianos, safes, and machinery.

Blow the Book Away

Move a book back and forth by blowing on it? Try it!

You need:
2 long pieces of string or rope
a book
a wooden hanger

WHAT TO DO:

Loop the two strings around the book and knot them. Then tie the loose ends of the strings to the rod of the wooden hanger so that the book swings freely, as in the illustration.

Blow on the book. Continue blowing on it every time it swings back toward you.

WHAT HAPPENS:

Even gentle blowing seems to make the book swing vigorously.

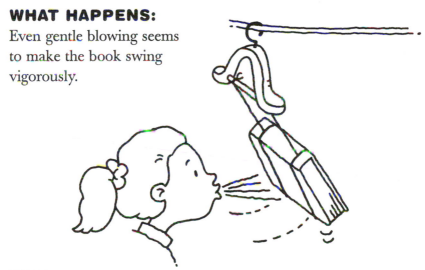

WHY:

It's not only a question of force but also one of timing. Even though you may not be blowing very hard, regular blowing at the right moment sends the book flying.

Swing Time

Galileo first performed this amazing experiment with strings in 1583!

You need:
4 strings of different lengths
2 strings of the same length
a clothesline or hanger
5 paper clips or metal nuts
a teaspoon

WHAT TO DO:

Tie the clips to five of the strings and attach a teaspoon to the sixth. Tie each string to the clothesline or hanger. Swing the teaspoon.

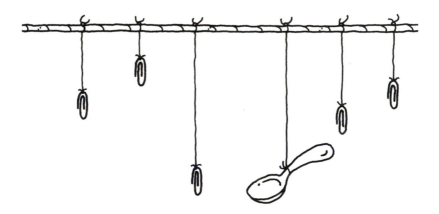

All the strings with the clips on them start to swing. But the clip on the string that's the same length as the string with the teaspoon swings with more energy than the others—and the string with the teaspoon winds down! Then the spoon string picks up vigor and the same-length string with the clip slows down!

WHY:

The swing of the teaspoon moves along the hanger and gives all the strings and the clips a push, starting them all moving. But each string, depending on its length, swings back and forth at a different time. Only one string with a clip–the one that swings at the same time as the teaspoon–gets pushed at the right moment to build up its swing. It swings with more vigor than the others until it loses energy to the teaspoon string, which builds up its swing again. The string with the teaspoon and the same-length string with the clip continue taking turns speeding up and slowing down.

Making a Sheet Bend

If your string or rope isn't long enough, use the sheet bend, a knot for joining two ropes.

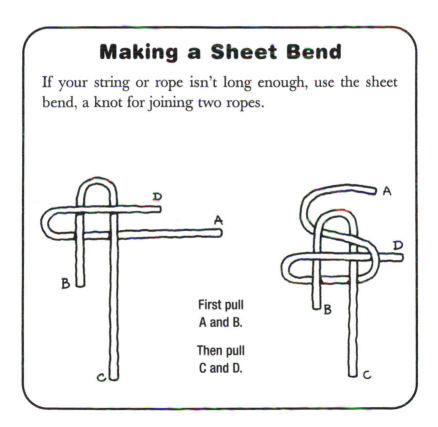

First pull
A and B.

Then pull
C and D.

A String Grandfather Clock

You can measure time with a string!

You need:

lengths of string or heavy thread:
 10 inches (25 cm), 20 inches (50 cm),
 39 inches (97.5 cm), 48 inches (120 cm)

a weight such as a metal washer or a coin

a clothes hanger (or ceiling hook)

a watch that indicates seconds

WHAT TO DO:

Tie a small weight to the 48-inch (120 cm) string and suspend it from a clothes hanger or ceiling hook. If you don't have a long enough string, you can use sheet bends (see p. 101) to link strings.

Pull the string slightly to one side and let it swing. Count the number of swings it makes in sixty seconds. Then pull the string farther over to one side and count the number of swings in sixty seconds. Jot down your results.

Now do the same thing with strings of different lengths: 10 inches (25 cm), 20 inches (50 cm), and finally 39 inches (97.5 cm). In each case, count the number of times the weight moves back and forth in sixty seconds, and write it down.

WHAT HAPPENS:

When the string is about 39 inches (97.5 cm) long, the weight moves back and forth 60 times in one minute.

WHY:

A pendulum takes the same amount of time to make every swing no matter how far it travels or how heavy the weight at the end of it. But the longer the pendulum, the longer the time it takes to complete its swing, and the shorter the pendulum, the more quickly it travels back and forth.

Since a length of string measuring 39 inches (97.5 cm) swings back and forth 60 times in one minute, you know that every complete swing it makes measures one second. You can use that length of string to measure time with great accuracy.

In 1673 Christopher Huygens used this principle in his design for a grandfather clock.

String Balance

You can make your own scale with a few strings and then put it to work weighing small objects.

You need:

3 strings of different lengths:
  4 inches (10 cm),
  6 inches (15 cm), and
  8 inches (20 cm)

a ruler about 12 inches (30 cm) long

tack or tape

a hanger

12 or so small paper clips

WHAT TO DO:

Attach the 6-inch (15 cm) string to the center of the ruler with a tack or tape, making sure that it won't come loose. Tie the free end of the string to the rod of the hanger, as in the illustration.

Attach the other two strings so that they are the same distance from the ends of the ruler. Knot the free ends of the strings.

Unbend one of the paper clips and shape it so that it fits tightly when you hang it over the ruler. Slide it along the ruler until the ruler hangs straight.

Link two of the other paper clips and tie them to the 8-inch (20 cm) length of string.

Then attach clips to the 4-inch (10 cm) string until the ruler is balanced again.

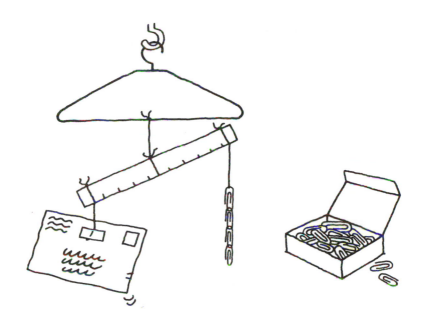

WHAT HAPPENS:

You need to attach four clips to the 4-inch (10 cm) string to balance the two clips attached to the 8-inch (20 cm) string.

WHY:

In the balance scale, the weight (two clips) multiplied by the length (8 inches [20 cm]) on one side must equal the weight (four clips) multiplied by the length (4 inches [10 cm]) on the other.

You can use your string scale to weigh various objects.

How many clips will you have to add to the 8-inch (20 cm) string if you attach a 1-ounce (28 g) letter to the 4-inch (10 cm) string? Once you find out, you can tell in one quick glance whether you've put enough postage on a letter.

SOAP SUDS

Make "blood," sink a ship, power a paper boat, move toothpicks at will, put bubbles to work—all with soap.

ABOUT SOAP

Ancient peoples used water and wood ashes to wash up and then soothed their clean but irritated bodies with grease or oil from animals or plants.

About two thousand years ago the Gauls invented a soap that combined wood ashes and animal fat. They used it to make their hair brighter.

A soap factory and bars of scented soap were found in the ruins of Pompeii, the city that was destroyed in the first century AD by a volcanic eruption.

Commercial soap makers combine fat or grease with lye (an alkali made from wood ash) and salt. They add perfumes, coloring, water softeners, and preservatives before they shape or flake the soap.

The word **detergent** means anything that will clean things. Most people today use the word to mean a cleaner manufactured from a man-made substance usually derived from petroleum. It was first developed for commercial use in the 1950s.

Dracula's Favorite Soap

Terrify your friends with this one!

You need:
a bar of soap
2 or 3 laxative pills, such as Ex-Lax or Feen-a-Mint
1 tablespoon of rubbing alcohol (15 mL)

WHAT TO DO:
Mash one or two pieces of Ex-Lax or Feen-a-Mint in a table-spoon of rubbing alcohol. Rub some of the solution on your hand and allow it to dry. Then wash it off with soap.

WHAT HAPPENS:
The soapy water turns bright red.

WHY:
The laxative contains a compound known as phenolph-thalein. This substance turns a brilliant red when it mixes with an alkali. Soap is made from fat boiled together with a strong alkali. When you add water, you free some of the alkali. This alkali mixes with the phenolphthalein on your hand—and turns your hand blood red.

Soapy Shipwreck

What does soap do to water that makes washing easier? Watch!

You need:

1 teaspoon liquid soap
  (either dishwashing soap
  or laundry detergent)

pin or needle
1 cup (240 mL) water
tweezer or hairpin

WHAT TO DO:

Float a pin on a cup of water. It's easier if you lower the pin with a pair of tweezers or a hairpin or even a fork. Then carefully add liquid soap drop by drop.

WHAT HAPPENS:

As you add soap, the pin sinks.

WHY:

To start with, the pin isn't actually floating. It is resting on the water's invisible elastic skin.

Water molecules are strongly attracted to one another and stick close together, especially on the surface of the water. This creates tension—enough tension to support an object you'd think would sink. Surface tension also prevents water from surrounding the particles of dirt, soot, and dust on your skin or clothes.

When dissolved in water, soap separates the water molecules, reducing the surface tension. That's why the pin sinks—and why soapy water washes dirt away.

Soap Power

Can you use soap to power a boat? Well, maybe a very small one—in a basin or in the bathtub.

You need:
a pinch of detergent
scissors
an index card
a pot of water

WHAT TO DO:
From an index card cut out a boat approximately 2 inches by 1 inch (5 cm x 2.5 cm), with a small slot for the "engine" in the rear, as in the illustration. Then float the boat in a pot of water. Pour a little detergent into the "engine" slot.

WHAT HAPPENS:
Your boat travels through the water.

WHY:
The soap breaks the water's elastic "skin," the surface tension (see page 109), behind the boat. The boat sails forward—and will stop only when the soap reduces the surface tension of all the water in your "lake."

Picky Toothpicks

Make a circle of toothpicks come and go at will.

You need:

a piece of soap
a bowl of water
a cube of sugar
6 toothpicks
  or matches

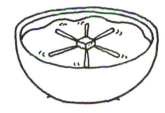

WHAT TO DO:

Arrange the toothpicks in a circle in a bowl of water. Place a cube of sugar in the center of the circle.

Change the water and arrange the toothpicks in a circle again. This time place a piece of soap in the center.

WHAT HAPPENS:

When you place sugar in the center, the toothpicks are drawn to it. When you place soap in the center, the toothpicks are repelled.

WHY:

The sugar sucks up water, creating a current that carries the toothpicks with it toward the center. The soap, on the other hand, gives off an oily film that spreads outward. It weakens the surface tension (page 109), and the film carries the toothpicks away with it.

Polluting the Duck Pond

Is anything wrong with washing your clothes with detergent in a lake or pond? Take a look!

You need:

liquid detergent

wax paper

felt-tipped pen (optional)

a plastic bag

a large pan or bowl of water

WHAT TO DO:

Stuff a plastic bag with bits of plastic or wax paper. Close it with its regular fastener or staple it closed. If you wish, draw a duck on the bag with a felt-tipped pen. Float your "duck" in the pan or bowl. Then add a little detergent.

WHAT HAPPENS:

The duck sinks.

WHY:

The wax paper and plastic are water-repellent—just the way a live duck is. A duck's feathers are oily. This oil repels water and helps a duck to float. But a detergent enables water to stick to greasy materials. Detergent may be fine for washing dishes and clothes, but it is deadly for the duck.

Handmade Bubbles

Bubbles are globs of air or gas inside a hollow liquid ball. Soap bubbles are globs of air enclosed in a film of soapy water. You can make bubbles by blowing through a pipe or a ring dipped in soapsuds. You can do it with just your hand, too.

You need:
2 tablespoons (30 mL) dishwashing liquid
1 cup (240 mL) warm water

WHAT TO DO:
Gently stir the dishwashing liquid into the warm water. Curl your fingers and dip your hand in the soapy mixture. Blow into your curled hand.

WHAT HAPPENS:
Bubbles form.

WHY:
When you blow into the mixture of water and detergent on your wet hand, you add the air that forms the center of the bubble.

Bubble Mix Recipes

Recipes for bubble mix differ, partly because soap powders and detergents vary in strength. Experiment and figure out which ones work best for you. Here are some suggestions that may help:

- Dishwashing detergent usually works well.
- Use at least 1 part soap to 8 to 10 parts of warm water for a normal mix. For example, use 1 tablespoon (15 mL) soap for every 1/2 cup water (125 mL) or 1/2 cup (120 mL) soap to 5 cups (1.25 L) water.
- A larger proportion of soap to water makes larger bubbles.
- More detergent than water creates giant bubbles.
- Add sugar, gelatin powder, or glycerin to get longer-lasting bubbles. Bubbles burst when they dry out. These substances slow down the evaporation of water that causes the drying out. Try 1 part sugar or gelatin or glycerin to 1 part soap and 6 parts water.

Bubble Tips

- Save clean jars of different sizes to hold your various bubble mixes.
- Stir gently so as not to whip up soapsuds. (Suds are actually tiny bubbles.)
- Let bubble mix stand for a day or two, if possible.
- Put the bubble mix in the refrigerator for a few minutes before using it. Your bubbles will last longer.
- For best results, blow bubbles on a rainy day. Because there is more moisture in the air, they will last longer.

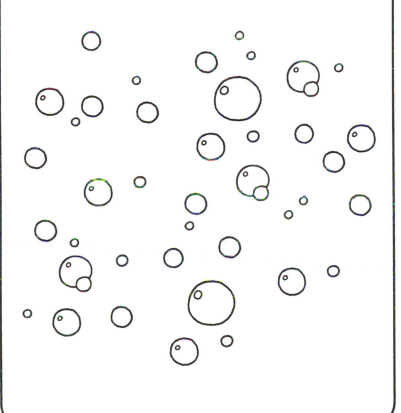

Making a Bubble Blower

You can make a bubble blower from a wire clothes hanger.

You need:

an uncoated wire hanger

a cylindrical object,
  such as a frozen juice can
  or thick crayon

WHAT TO DO:

Make a ring by untwisting the wire hanger and then wrapping a piece of it around the can. Slip the can out. Leave 3 or 4 inches (7.5–10 cm) of straight wire for a handle. Then bend the rest of the wire back and forth until it snaps, and you have your bubble wand.

Dip it in bubble mix and wave it in the air.

WHAT HAPPENS:

You get a spray of bubbles.

WHY:

By waving the soapy wand in the air, you add the air that forms the center of the bubble.

Other Bubble Blowers

You can make a bubble blower from almost anything: a soda straw, a clay pipe, a tin or plastic horn, a funnel, a paper cup with the end removed, a juice can with both ends removed, a cut-away plastic bottle, and more!

Super Bubble

To create a large bubble, you need a large bubble blower and a strong bubble mix.

You need:

2 drinking straws (plastic ones are stronger)
a jar of bubble mix with more detergent than water (see p. 114)
3 feet (90 cm) of string
a large baking pan

WHAT TO DO:

Thread the string through the two drinking straws and tie the ends of the string to one another. Pour the bubble mix into a large baking pan or tray. Wetting your fingers first, hold one straw in each hand and dip the strings and straws into the mixture for a couple of seconds.

Remove the strings from the mix and pull the straws apart so that the string is taut. Holding the straws as though they were a frame, wave them around several times. Then pull the straws upward and bring them close together.

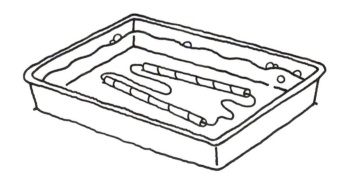

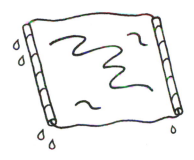

WHAT HAPPENS:

You release an enormous round bubble.

WHY:

You get a large bubble because you are adding a large amount of air when you wave the straw frame and pull the straws up. As this air pushes out in all directions, you pull apart the molecules of the soapy film. But the molecules are attracted to one another, and the elastic skin of the bubble contracts as much as it can to form the smallest surface for the air it contains. The form that has the smallest surface is the sphere. That's why the bubble is round.

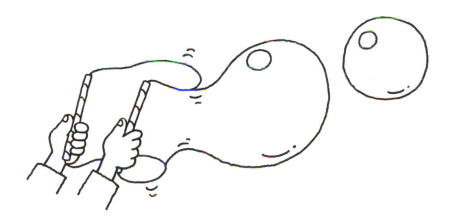

Bubble Duet

Blow two bubbles with one bubble blower—and see how they affect each other.

You need:
a plastic drinking straw
scissors
a bowl of bubble mix

WHAT TO DO:

Cut four slits about 2/3 inch (1.5 cm) long at both ends of a plastic drinking straw. Bend the cut strips outward, as in the illustration. Make a small slit in the middle of the straw, and bend it at the slit. You have now created a two-ended bubble pipe.

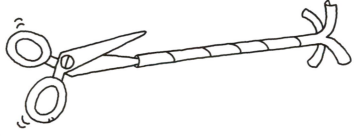

Dip one end of the pipe into the bubble mix and blow into the middle slit. You'll get a bubble. Blow a second bubble by dipping the other end of your pipe into the mix and blowing through the middle slit again.

Then seal the slit in the middle of the bubble pipe by covering it with your fingers.

WHAT HAPPENS:

When you blow the second bubble, the first one gets larger. When the opening is sealed, the smaller second bubble gets even smaller while the first one gets even larger.

WHY:

Because a small bubble is more curved than a large bubble, the air pressure exerted by its elastic skin is greater than that on a large bubble. Therefore, the small bubble gets smaller. The air from it is forced into the bigger bubble, which then gets even larger.

Bubble Stand

To make a stand for your bubbles, all you need to do is place a plastic cup or container upside down.

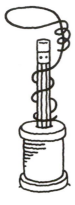

Or you can place a pencil in the hole of a wooden spool of thread and wind a wire loop about it, as in the illustration at the left

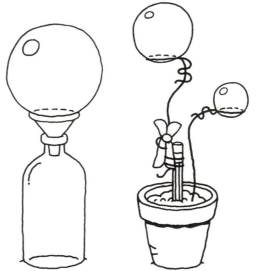

Transfer a bubble from a bubble blower to the stand by simply shaking it off gently. You can then observe the bubble—and make others.

Rainbow in a Bubble

A rainbow in a bubble? Yes!

You need:

a bubble blower,
  such as a wire ring

1 tablespoon (15 mL) sugar

bubble mix

a refrigerator

a bubble stand

WHAT TO DO:

Add the sugar to the bubble mix. Place the solution in the refrigerator for a few minutes. This will make the bubbles last longer.

Dip the bubble blower into the mix. When you have a film of soap on the ring, blow gently. Attach your bubble to the bubble stand by shaking the bubble blower over the stand.

WHAT HAPPENS:

After a few minutes, you see different colors.

WHY:

When light hits a bubble, most of it passes through it because the bubble is transparent. But as the air in it evaporates and the bubble gets even thinner, some of the rays that make up white light don't pass through. Instead, thy are reflected back from either the inside or the outside. That's why you see various colors of the spectrum. The colors change and disappear, because the bubble's thickness is not the same all over and is constantly changing.

Bubble in a Bubble in a Bubble

Use your bubble stand to put a bubble in your bubble's bubble.

You need:

a plastic cup or other bubble stand
bubble mix
a bubble ring or other bubble

blower
a straw

WHAT TO DO:

Wet the top of a plastic cup or the wire loop of a bubble stand. Blow a large soap bubble with the wire ring and attach it to the bubble stand. Wet a plastic straw in the bubble mix and put it through the large bubble. Blow a smaller bubble inside the large one.

Then carefully push the straw through your smaller bubble, and blow an even smaller one.

WHAT HAPPENS:

You get a bubble in a bubble in a bubble.

WHY:

Anything wet can penetrate the bubble without breaking it. The wet surface coming into contact with the soapy film becomes part of it. Don't touch the wet wall with your smaller bubble or you won't get a separate bubble.

Putting a Bubble to Work

We can make an ordinary soap bubble do work for us!

You need:

an empty thread spool
a 3-inch (7.5 cm) square of paper
a ½-inch (1–1.5 cm) cork
bubble mix
a long needle

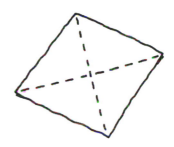

WHAT TO DO:

Stick a needle through the cork, point up. Place the cork on a level surface such as a table or desk.

Fold the paper diagonally twice. Unfold it. Balance the center of the paper square (where the creases meet) on the point of the needle, as in the drawing.

Dip the spool in the bubble mix and blow a bubble on one end. Hold the other end toward the paper.

WHAT HAPPENS:

The paper moves.

WHY:

Air escaping from the bubble moves the paper.

Take a Bubble Dancing

Think your bubbles have worked hard enough? Do they need a little recreation? Take them dancing!

You need:
a comb
a piece of flannel or wool
a wire or other bubble blower
bubble mix

WHAT TO DO
Rub a comb several times against a piece of flannel or wool. Float bubbles above the fabric so that they land on it. Then move the charged comb close to each of the bubbles in turn.

WHAT HAPPENS:
Each bubble seems to dance—moving up and then falling down.

WHY:
You are using static electricity—electricity created by friction—to make your bubbles "dance."

By rubbing the comb on the material, you charge it with static electricity. Because charges of electricity that are not alike attract one another, the charged comb attracts the uncharged bubbles. The bubbles become charged by the comb and are pushed away, because they now have the same charge of static electricity as the comb. Charges of electricity that are alike repel each other. Each time the bubbles come up and touch the comb they get charged, and each time they go down they lose their charge and are pulled up again.

INDEX